# Mel Bay's SCHOOL OF Mandolin

## Blues

by Joe Carr

## CD track listing

| | |
|---|---|
| Tuning Notes ............................................. 1 | Turnaround #6 ......................................... 22 |
| 4/4-12/8 ................................................... 2 | Introduction #1 ....................................... 23 |
| Monotonic Blues Shuffle .......................... 3 | Introduction #2 ....................................... 24 |
| Blues Shuffle #1 ....................................... 4 | Introduction #3 ....................................... 25 |
| 4/4 Blues ................................................... 5 | Introduction #4 ....................................... 26 |
| Flat Seven Shuffle .................................... 6 | *Introduction #5* ..................................... 27 |
| Two Note Blues ......................................... 7 | *Joe's Blues* ............................................ 28 |
| Chords ...................................................... 8 | Creating a Blues Solo ............................. 29 |
| D/G Scales ................................................ 9 | Creating a Blues Solo - Part Two ........... 30 |
| Paired Grids ............................................ 10 | Creating a Blues Solo - Part Three ......... 31 |
| A/E Scale ................................................ 11 | Creating a Blues Solo - Part Four ........... 32 |
| C Scale ................................................... 12 | *Saint James Infirmary* .......................... 33 |
| *Monroe's Blues #1* ............................... 13 | *Saint James Infirmary* - Notes .............. 34 |
| *Monroe's Blues #2* ............................... 14 | *Saint James Infirmary* - Solo ............... 35 |
| *Yank's Blues* ........................................ 15 | *Jethro's Blues* ....................................... 36 |
| *Yank's Ragtime Blues* .......................... 16 | *Tiny's Blues* .......................................... 37 |
| Turnaround #1 ........................................ 17 | Jazz Progression #1 ................................ 38 |
| Turnaround #2 ........................................ 18 | Jazz Progression #2 ................................ 39 |
| Turnaround #3 ........................................ 19 | Jazz Progression #3 ................................ 40 |
| Turnaround #4 ........................................ 20 | *Johnny's Blues* ..................................... 41 |
| Turnaround #5 ........................................ 21 | |

1 2 3 4 5 6 7 8 9 0

© 2009 BY MEL BAY PUBLICATIONS, INC., PACIFIC, MO 63069.
ALL RIGHTS RESERVED. INTERNATIONAL COPYRIGHT SECURED. B.M.I. MADE AND PRINTED IN U.S.A.
No part of this publication may be reproduced in whole or in part, or stored in a retrieval system, or transmitted in any form
or by any means, electronic, mechanical, photocopy, recording, or otherwise, without written permission of the publisher.

**Visit us on the Web at www.melbay.com — E-mail us at email@melbay.com**

# Contents

| | |
|---|---|
| Introduction | 2 |
| Blues Rhythm and Chords | 3 |
| *Monotonic Blues Shuffle* | 4 |
| *Blues Shuffle #1* | 5 |
| *4/4 Blues* | 6 |
| *Flat Seven Shuffle* | 7 |
| Two Note Chords | 8 |
| Basic Chords | 9 |
| Major and Blues Scales | 10-11 |
| Black and White Blues - *Monroe's #1* | 12 |
| *Monroe's Blues #2* | 13 |
| *Yank's Blues* | 14 |
| *Yank's Ragtime Blues* | 15 |
| Turnarounds | 16-17 |
| Introductions | 18-19 |
| *Joe's Blues* | 20 |
| Creatiing a Blues Solo | 21-22 |
| Creating a Blues Solo - Part Two | 23 |
| Creating a Blues Solo - Part Three | 24 |
| Creating a Blues Solo - Part Four | 25 |
| *Saint James Infirmary* | 26 |
| *Saint James Infirmary* - Solo | 27 |
| *Jethro's Blues* | 28 |
| *Tiny's Blues* | 29 |
| Jazz Blues Progressions | 30 |
| *Johnny's Blues* | 31 |
| About the Author | 32 |

## School of Mandolin - Blues

This multi-volume series is designed to introduce beginning to intermediate mandolin players to a variety of essential techniques and common instructive tunes. The object in this series is to ground players in good technique and to impart the essential skills required for continued self-guided development. Other volumes in this series cover various specific styles including bluegrass, fiddle tunes, Italian favorites and classics.

While the mandolin is not as synonymous with the blues as the guitar, the fiddle's fretted cousin was an important lead voice in many string blues bands of the 1920s through the 1940s including the Mississippi Sheiks, the Memphis Jug Band and the Dallas String Band. In the hands of great players including Carl Martin, Charlie McCoy, Yank Rachell, Howard Armstrong and Johnny Young, the mandolin was a convincing member of the blues ensemble.

Several factors combined to make the mandolin a popular choice for rural southern blues players. Its similarity to the violin made the mandolin accessible to musicians familiar with violin tuning. The small mandolin traveled well and was affordable and readily available from a number of large retail sources. The mandolin's ability to play chords makes it an excellent choice for lead and accompaniment. Due to its high tuning as compared to the guitar, it was a great musical duet partner, especially when the guitar provides accompaniment with the mandolin taking the lead role.

White and black performers alike recognized the blues potential of the mandolin. In addition to the performers listed above, Bluegrass music innovator Bill Monroe developed a personal mandolin style that drew heavily from the blues tradition. Blues also played an important role in the styles of Leo Raley (Cliff Bruner's Texas Wanderers,) Jethro Burns (Homer and Jethro,) Tiny Moore (Bob Wills' Texas Playboys) and Johnny Gimble. Players such as Rich Delgrosso keep the blues mandolin tradition alive today

## Tuning Notes - G, D, A, E

# Blues Rhythm and Chords

Playing rhythm on the mandolin is the quickest and easiest way to join a jam session and start having fun playing now. With only a few chords, you will be able to play along with the most advanced lead players. Everyone needs a good rhythm player.

If you are a complete beginner, refer to for Mel Bay's School of Mandolin (MB21673BCD) for guidance with basic open chords. The goal of this chapter is to present chords and rhythm as used by blues musicians.

A very popular form of the blues is called the *12 bar blues*. This name refers to the 12 measures (bars) in 4/4 time of music that form the skeleton of many blues songs. In a measure of 4/4 music there are four beats. A basic blues chord progression could be written like this where each letter stands for four beats.

G C G G
C C G G
D C G (D)

The final measure in parenthesis above is called the *turnaround*. It accurately describes this measure that is used to send the song back to the beginning of the progression for another verse or a lead solo. If the song was ending here, another G chord would be used instead of the turnaround chord, D.

# The 12/8 Blues *Feel (The Shuffle)*

Although the blues can be written in 4/4 time, the *feel* of the music is often that of 12/8. To understand this, tap your foot to a count of four. While tapping your foot, count out loud "*ONE, two, three, FOUR, five, six.*" For each beat of your foot, you have counted three eighth notes. The foot tap occurs as you are saying *ONE* and *FOUR*.

In the music below there are two measures of music. The first measure is in 4/4 time followed by a measure of 12/8. To play the first measure accurately, count *one and two and three and four and* - resulting in eight eighth notes. This approach results in very square sounding music unless it is played with the unwritten blues feel. To play measure two, count *ONE, two, THREE, FOUR, five, SIX, SEVEN, eight, NINE, TEN, eleven, TWELVE*. On the capitalized numbers, you should play the notes. This long-short, long, short feel occurs in most blues music. It is often called the blues *shuffle*. Listen to the CD carefully. The music in this volume is written in 4/4 and 12/8. Some musical ideas are easier to read and write in one time signature over another. When there are two possibilities, the most clear presentation is used.

# Monotonic Blues Shuffle

Texas blues guitarist Mance Lipscomb (1895-1976) was known for a rhythm style called *monotonic* bass. Here we use his one note bass pattern on a basic three chord 12 bar blues. The open third (D) and fourth (G) strings sounded together in measure one are the one and five notes of a G scale and make a powerful sounding G chord. Likewise, in measure two, we have a two note C chord at the fifth fret and D at the seventh (measure nine.) The D chord in measure twelve is the turnaround.

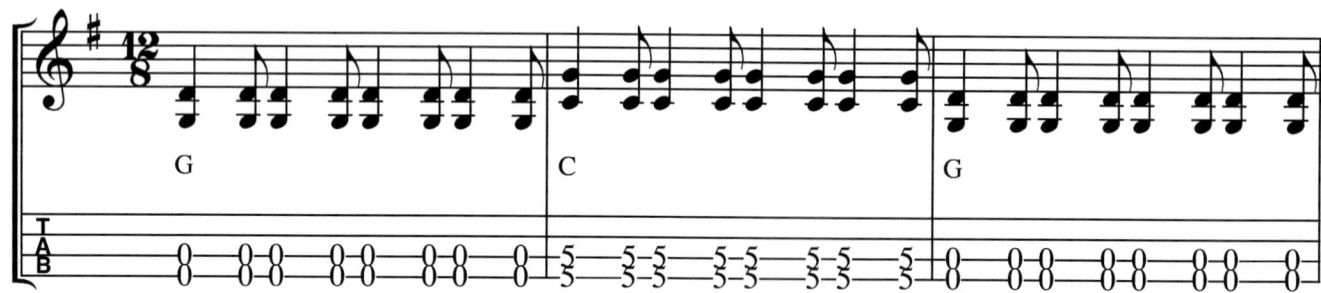

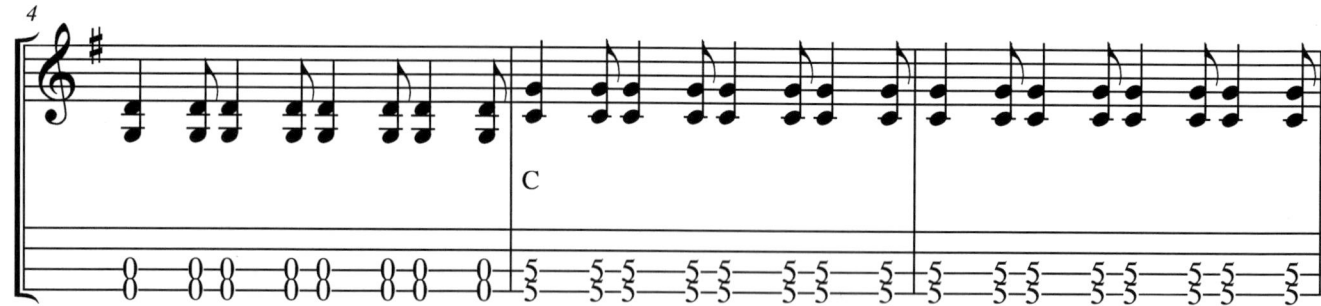

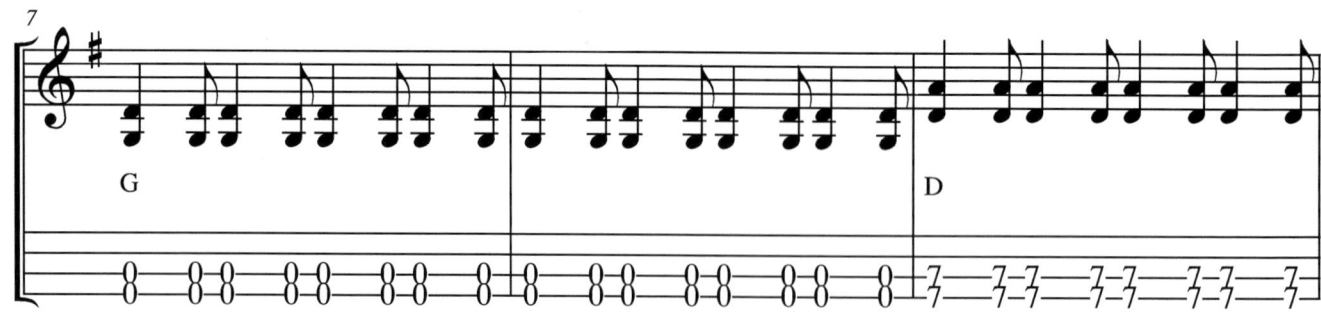

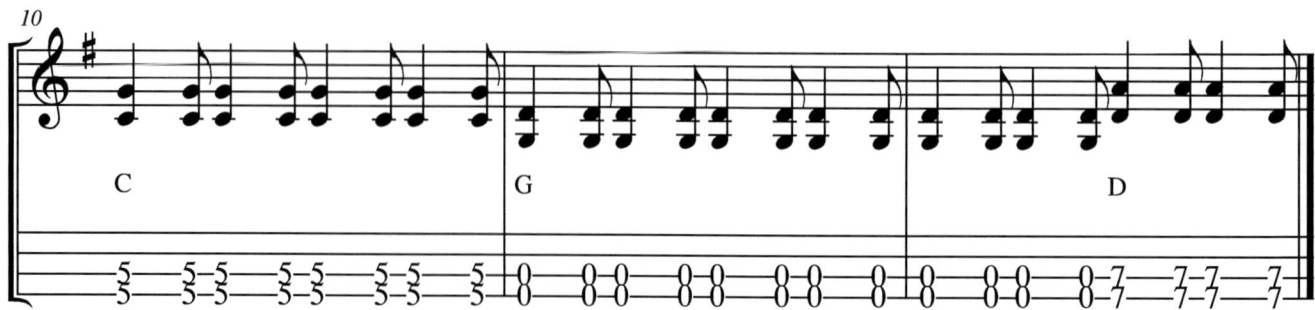

# Blues Shuffle #1

By changing the last bass notes of each measure we get this very recognizable blues shuffle pattern. It can be used as rhythm behind a singer or a solo or it can be played as a solo itself.

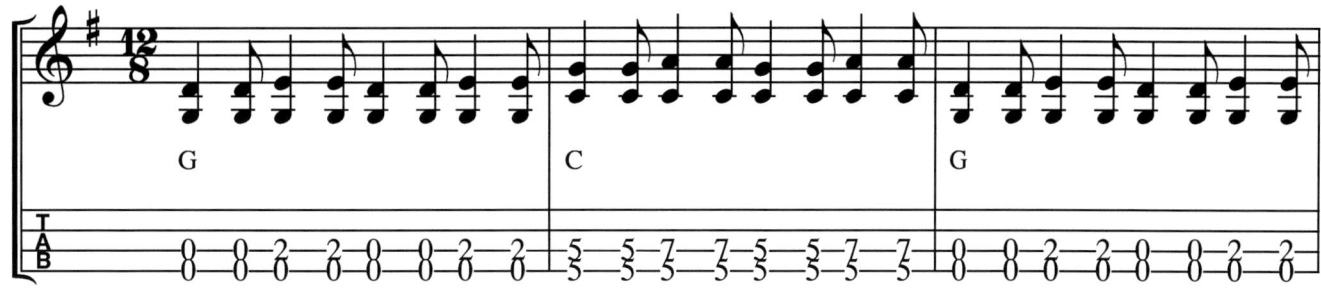

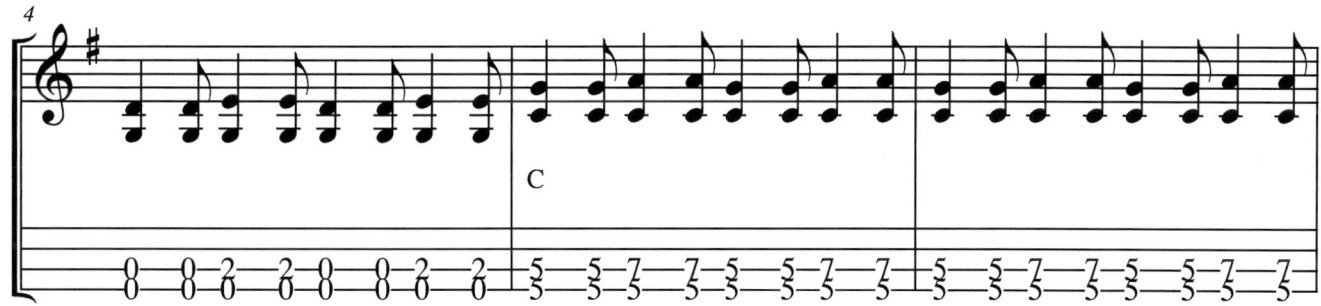

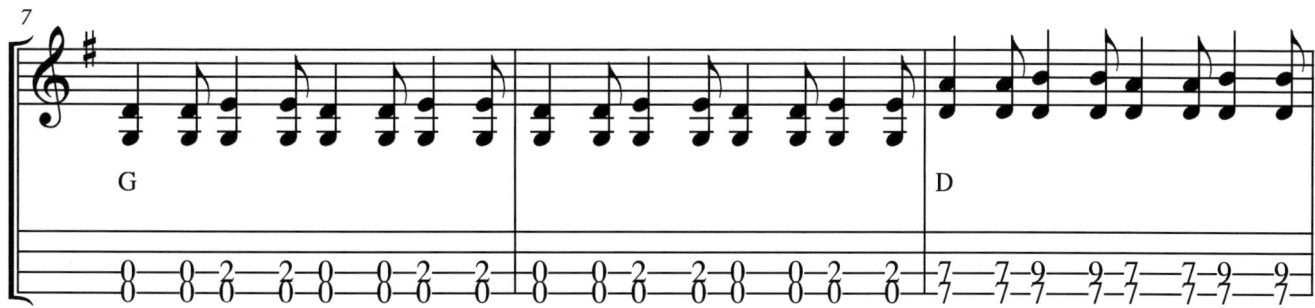

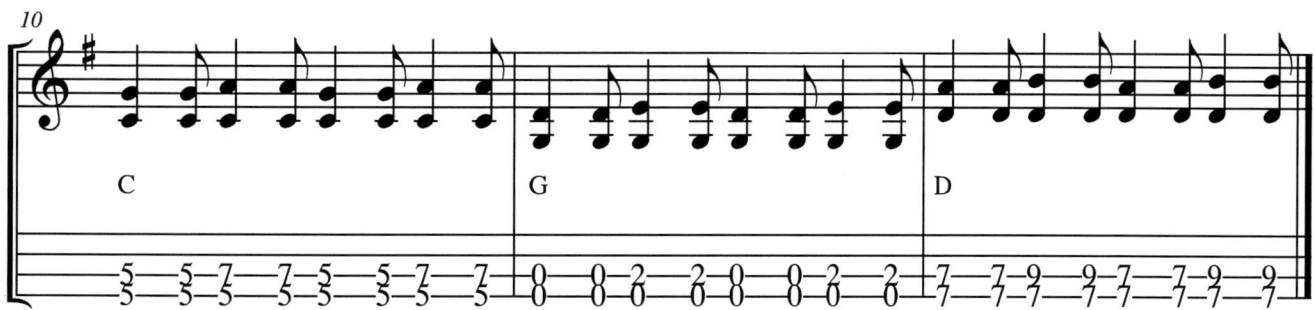

# The 4/4 Blues

Here is the previous example written in the standard 4/4 time. The letter "C" stands for *common* or 4/4 time. Remember to play this example with the 12/8 feel. In measures 11-12 we have our first lead turnaround. Play this entire exercise with downstrokes of the pick.

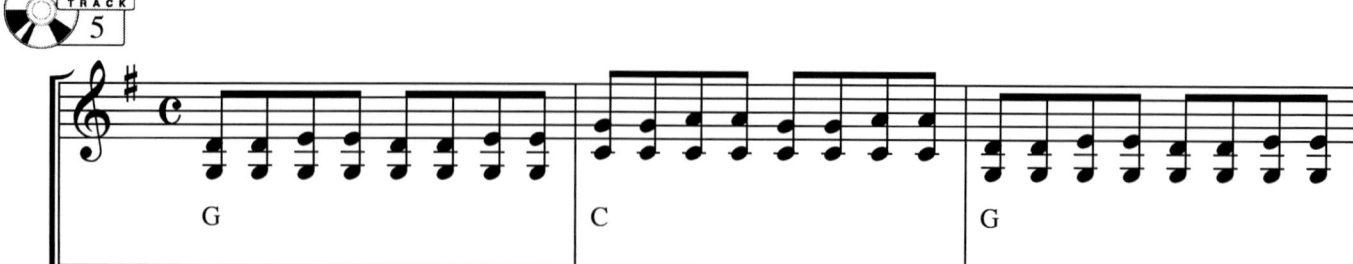
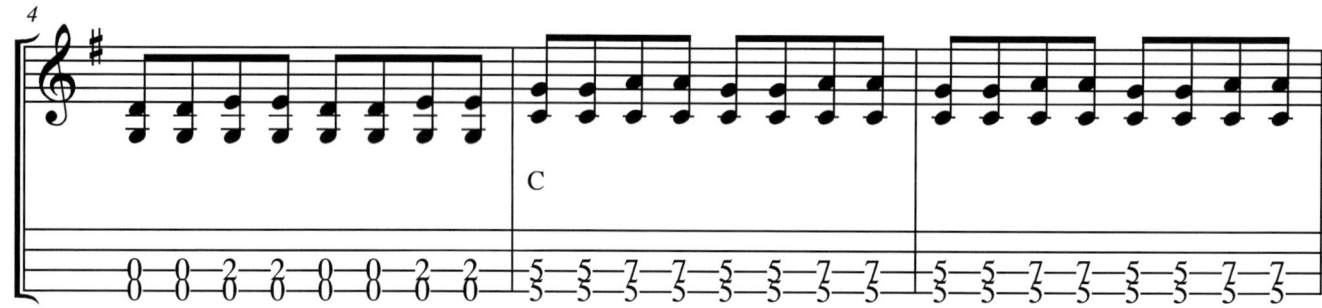
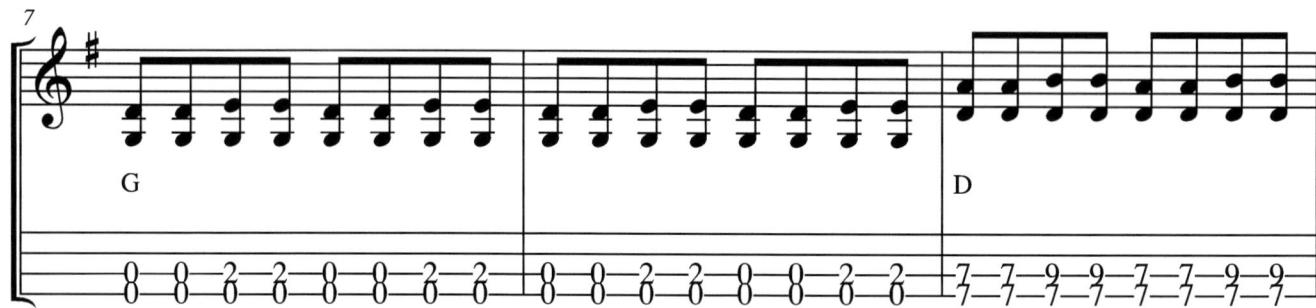

# Flat Seven Shuffle

By simply adding the flat seven note to the pattern (notes five and six in each measure) we get another familiar sound. The classic guitar instrumental *Honky Tonk* is built on this pattern.

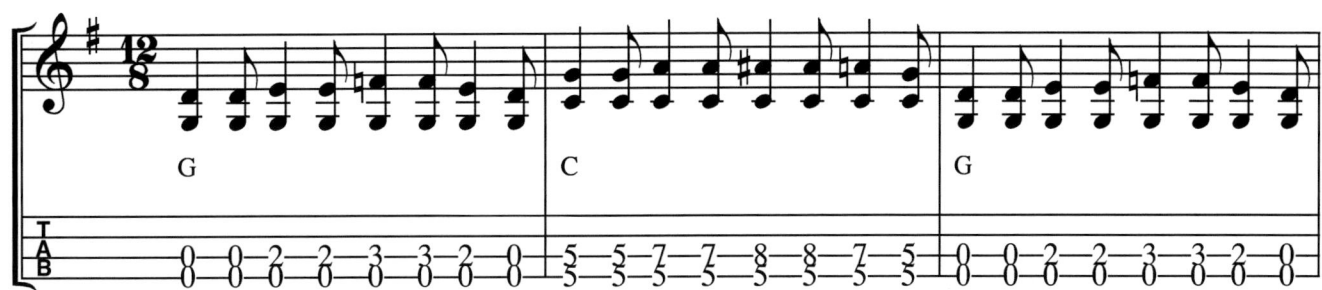

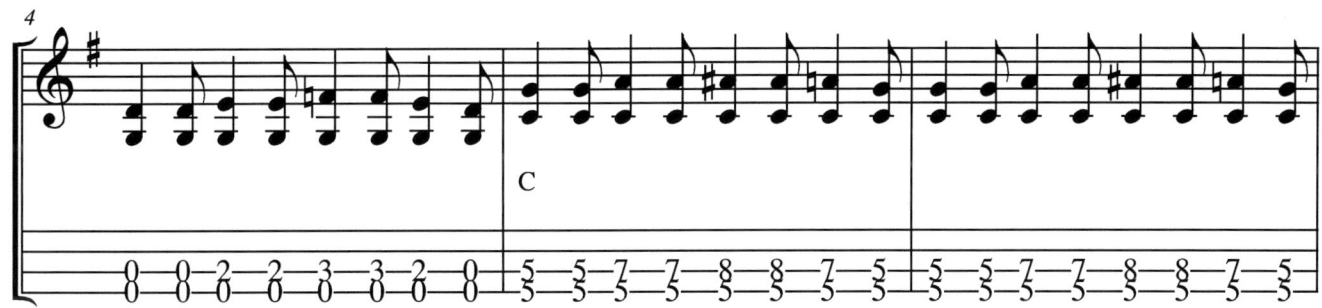

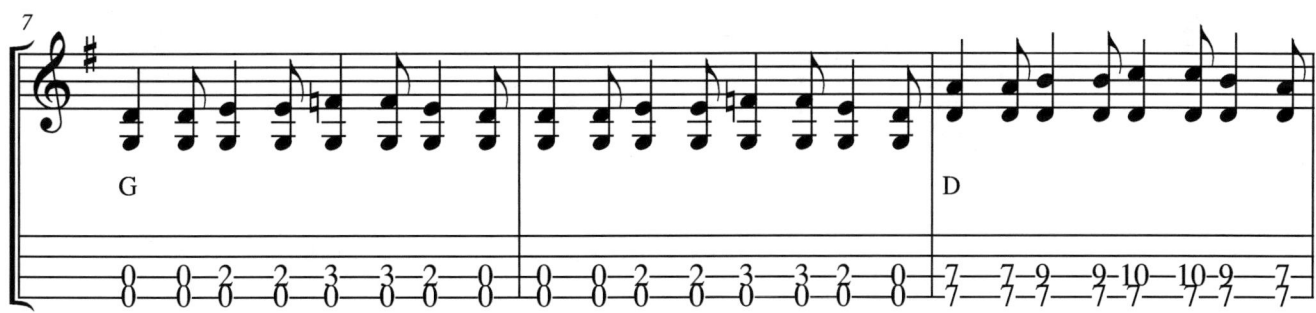

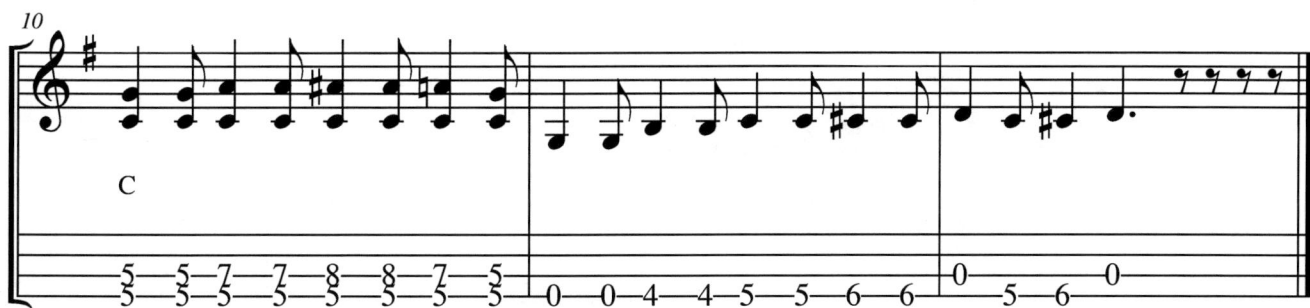

# Two Note Chords

The unique fifths tuning of the mandolin makes for many symmetrical chords and scales. The following progression uses a single shape for the D7, G7 and A7 chords. The change between each chord only takes moving one fret. The black dots in the diagram below indicate the open A (2nd) string that can be played with this example.

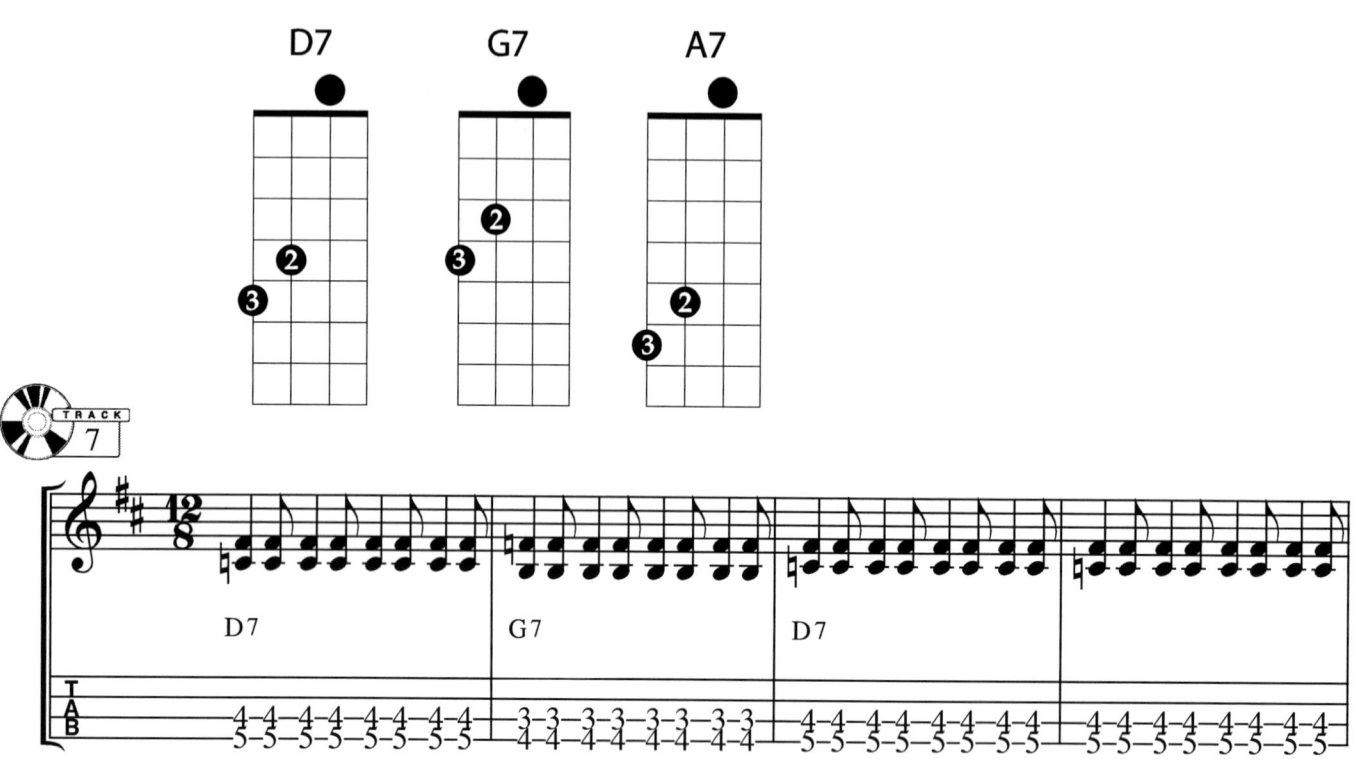

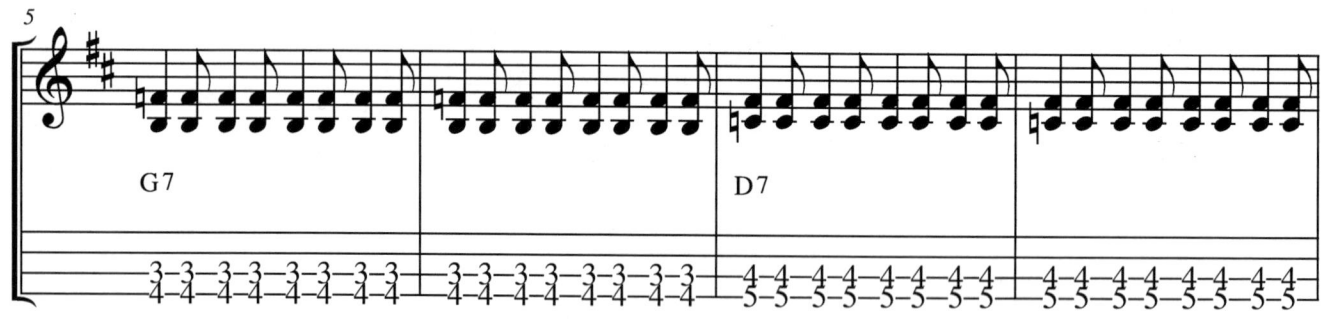

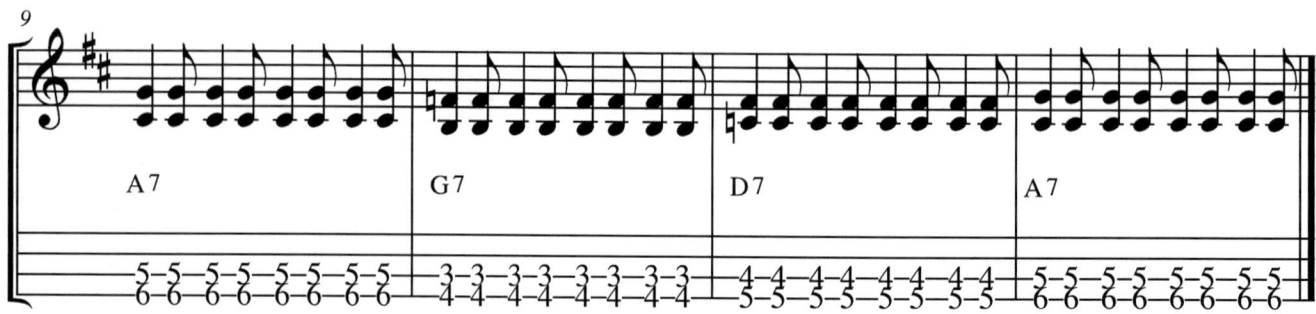

# Basic Chords

Here are some basic major, minor and seventh chords.

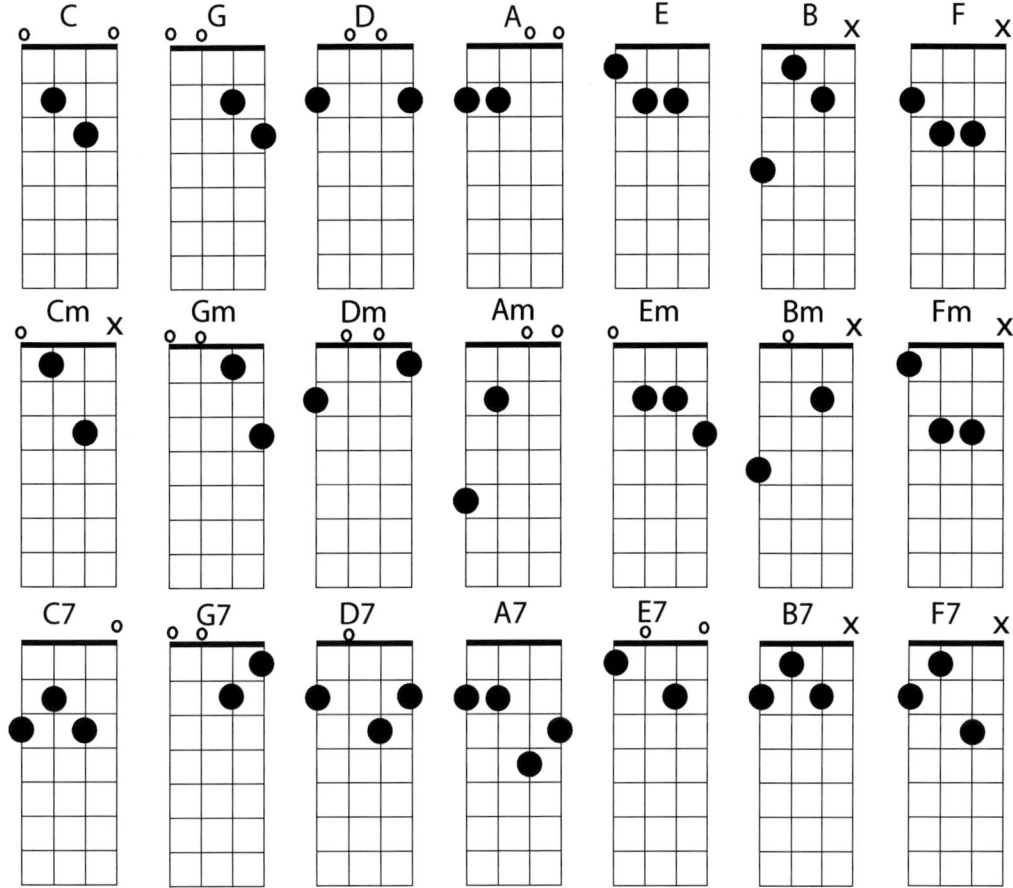

The three basic chords in a standard blues are called the one, four and five chords. The numbers come from the notes of the home scale. For example, the C scale is C-1, D-2, E-3, F-4, G-5, A-6, B-7, C-1. Therefore, F is the four chord and G is the five chord. In the blues, the five chord is usually played as a seventh. Using this chart, you can find the three basic chords (1, 4, 5) for the blues in the keys of C, G, D, A and E.

Key of C = (1) C, (4) F, (5) G7 - scale = C D E F G A B C
Key of G = (1) G, (4) C, (5) D7 - scale = G A B C D E F♯ G (one sharp)
Key of D = (1) D, (4) G, (5) A7 - scale = D E F♯ G A B C♯ D (two sharps)
Key of A = (1) A, (4) D, (5) E7 - scale = A B C♯ D E F♯ G♯ A (three sharps)
Key of E = (1) E, (4) A, (5) B7 - scale = E F♯ G♯ A B C♯ D♯ E (four sharps)

# Using the Flat Seven (Dominant) Chord in the Blues

In most popular music, the flat seven or dominant chord can be used in two places in a progression. Most commonly it is used on the five chord. It can also be used on the one chord as a preparation when moving to the four chord. In the blues, the seventh chord can be used for all three chords (1. 4. 5) in the progression at the players discretion. A simple G (1,) C (4,) D (5) progrssion could be played G, C, D7 or G, C7, D7 or even G7, C7, D7. The two note chord blues on page eight is an example.

# Major and Blues Scales

In measures one and two below is a D major scale. In measures three and four is a D blues scale. In the second staff there are the same two scales in G. Notice the similarity of the two staves. They both begin with this major scale pattern: 0245, 0245, 0235. The blues scale begins: 0356, 035, 1345. Recognizing these patterns allows for quicker memorization.

The D blues scale in measure three uses the following scale notes 1, ♭3, 4, ♭5, 5, ♭7, 1 ♭3, 3, 4, 5. The "blue" notes in the scale are the flat (♭) three and the flat seven. These are the notes that give a song the "blues" sound. It is very important therefore to know where the three and seven notes are in every scale to get an authentic blues sound.

## Paired Grids

Each pair of grids below iilustrates two scales that share the same fingerings. The D and G pair (in the middle) are written in notation on the staves above. The D blues scale is on strings 3, 2 and 1. Simply move the pattern to strings 4, 3 and 2 for the G blues scale.

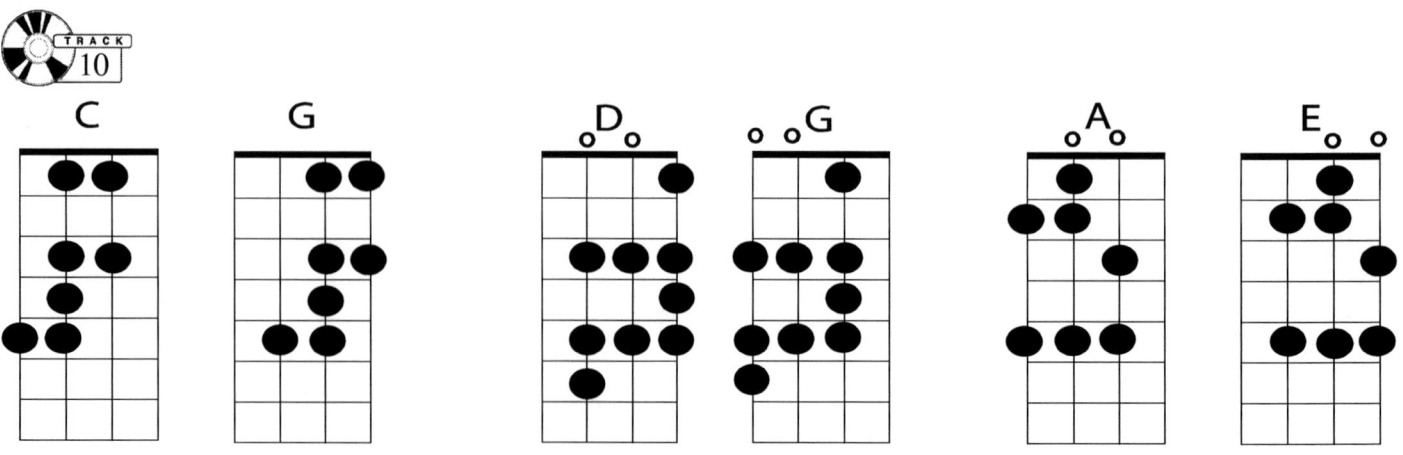

## A and E Scales

Here are the A nd E major and blues scales. As before, the A scales on strings 4, 3 and 2 become E scales when they are moved to strings 3, 2 and 1.

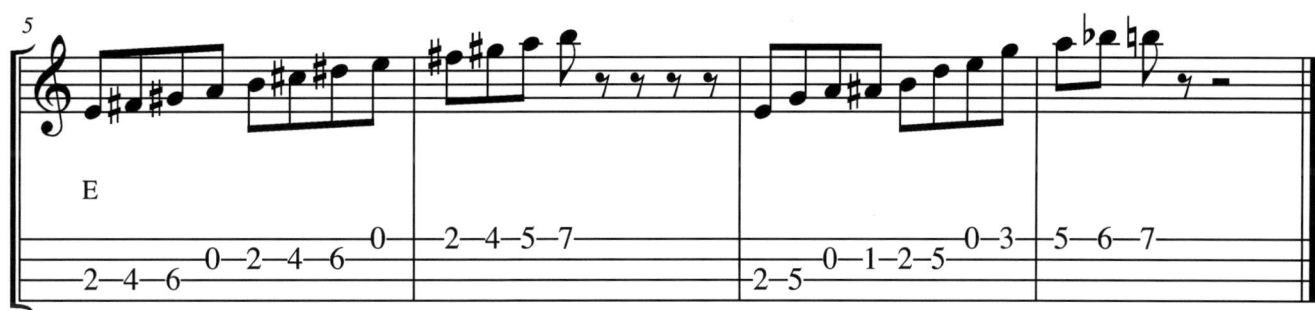

## C Scale

Here are the C major and blues scales. It pairs with the G scale when it is moved from strings 4, 3 and 2 to strings 3, 2 and 1.

# Black and White Blues

White musicians of the 1920s and 30s adopted and adapted the blues performed and recorded by black musicians. Many of the songs of Southern white performers in this period including Jimmie Rodgers, the Carter family, the Delmore Brothers, Sam and Kirk Magee, Bob Wills, the Monroe Brothers and many others, were learned from the playing of black musicians.

The white blues performance style was notably different, however. Generally, it can be observed that white performers tended to play the blues with a heavy 4/4 beat and did not use the eighth note triplet feel so obvious in much of the blues performed by black musicians. The mandolin music of Bluegrass music founder Bill Monroe is a good example.

*Monroe Blues #1* features on a strong quarter note, downbeat feel. Some of Monroe's original blues instrumentals were called *Stomps*, presumably referring to the strong 4/4 beat. These may have been intended as dance numbers. The progression is: GGGG
CCGG
DDGG

## Monroe's Blues #1

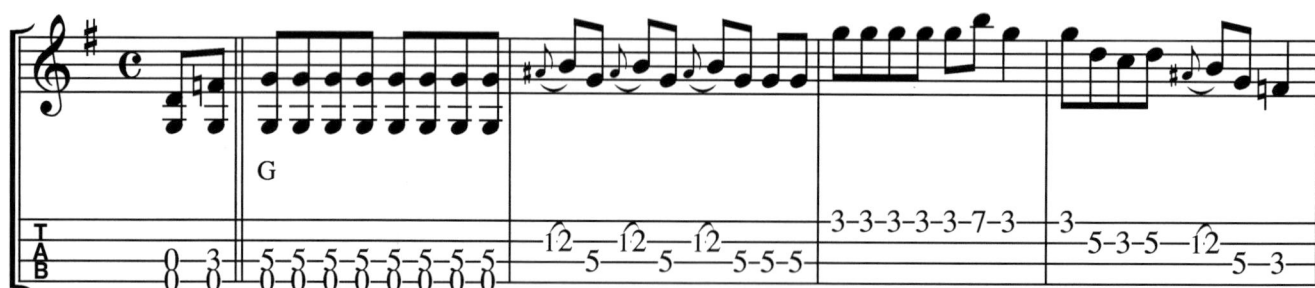

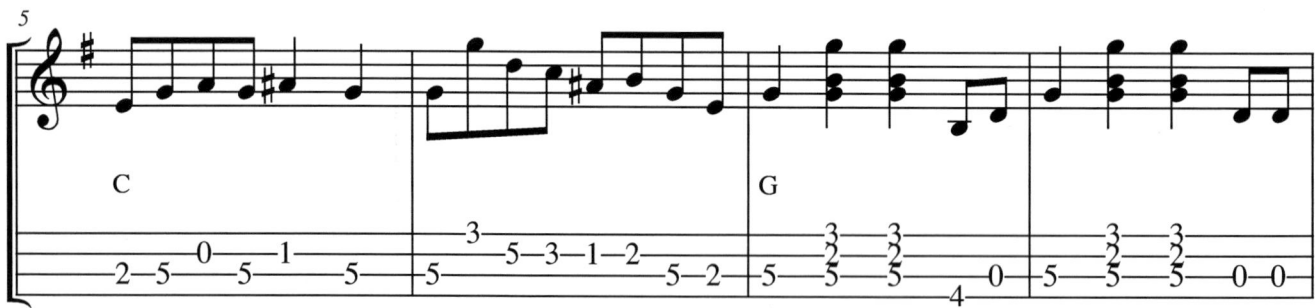

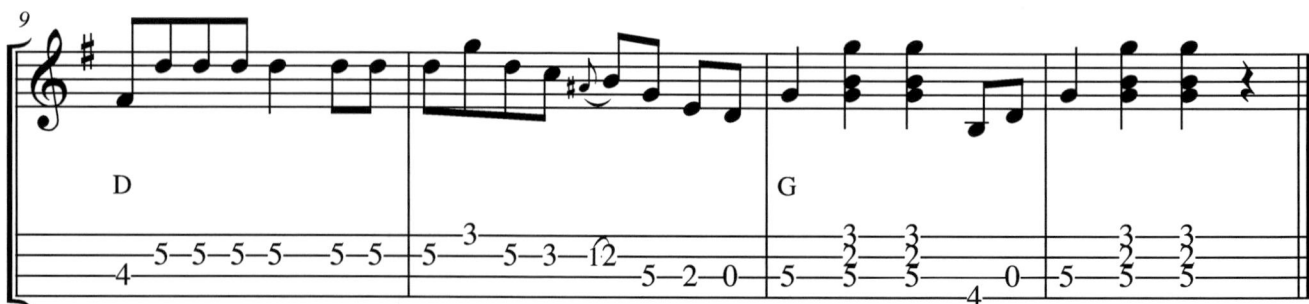

# Monroe's Blues #2

Here is a Monroe style bluegrass blues in the key of A.  Notice the open D note in measure nine is the flat seven note of the E chord.

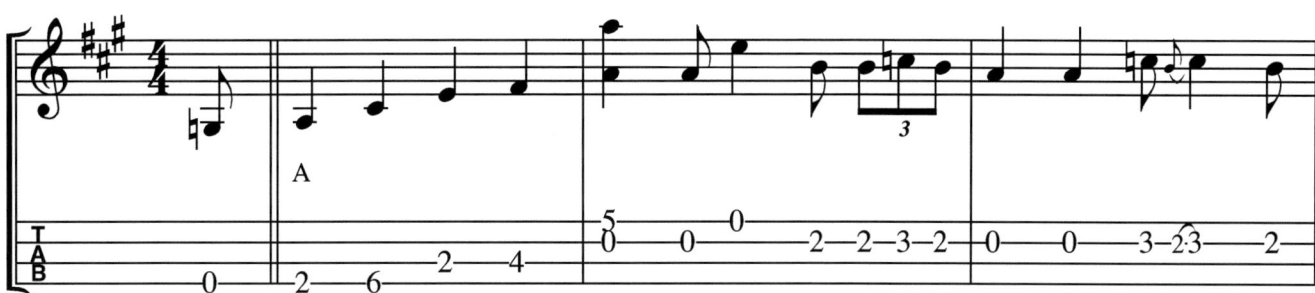

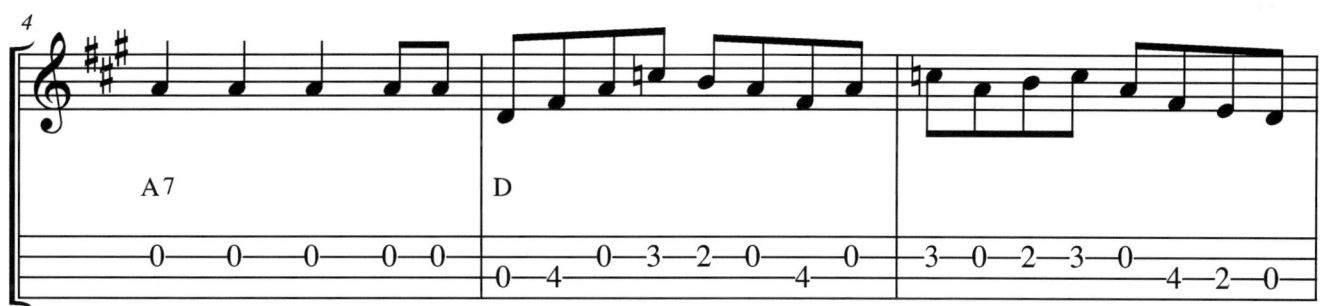

# Yank's Blues

In stark contrast to *Monroe's Blues #1* is this blues in the style of blues mandolin pioneer Yank Rachell. It is written in 12/8 to better convey the triplet eighth note feel that is used throughout. This blues should be played slower than *Monroe's Blues #1*.

The progression is:  GGGG
CCGG
DCGG

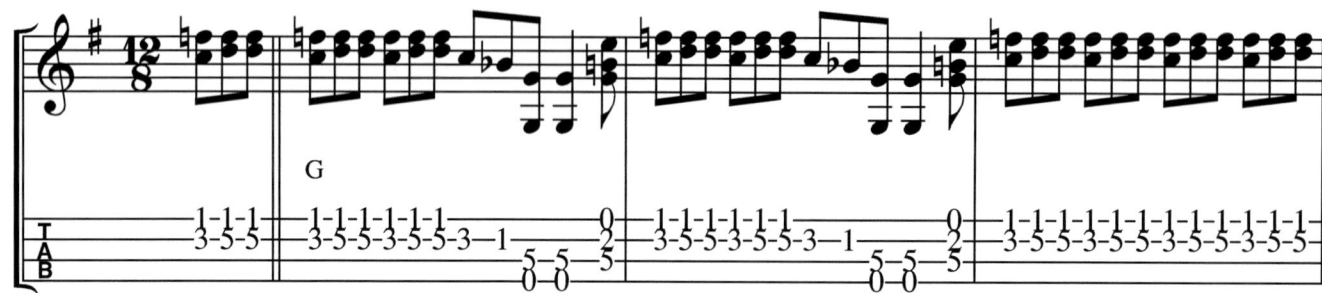

# Yank's Ragtime Blues

Here is an uptempo blues in the style of Rachell. The use of the dissonant half step in measure three is a common musical figure in ragtime.

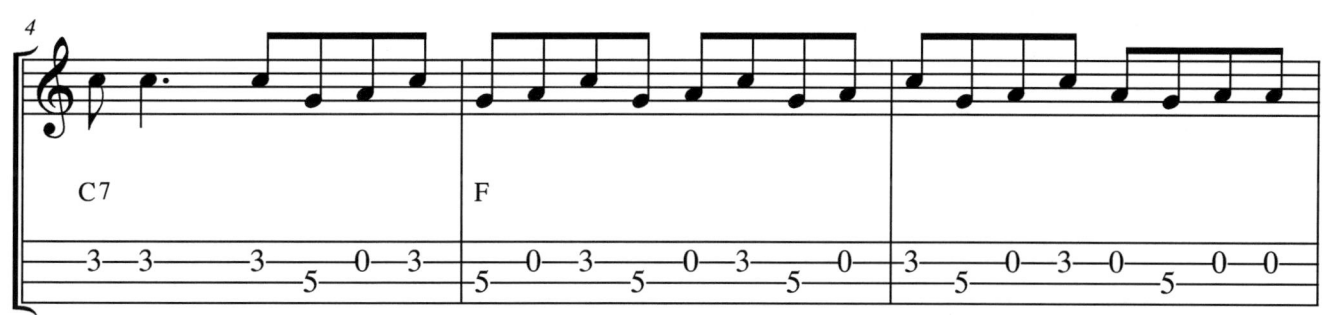
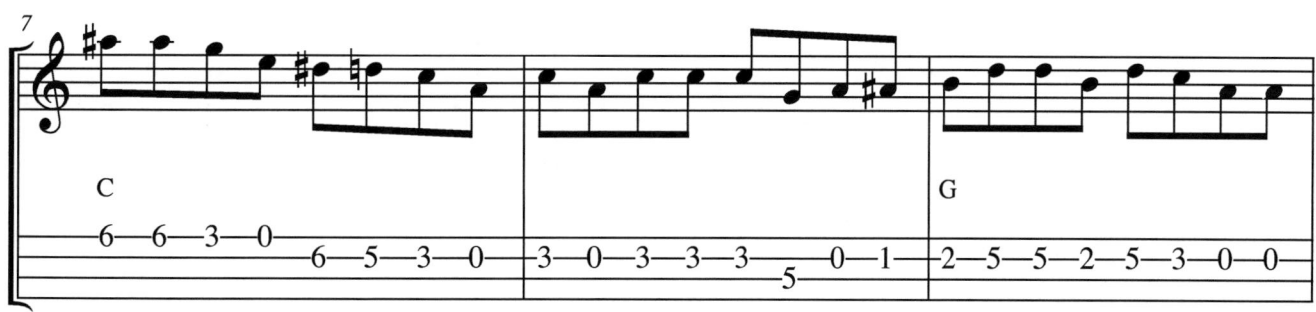

# Turnarounds

With the shuffle blues, we learned the final measure is often a turnaround. Using the G blues scale, here are some lead turnarounds. The first one features the F natural (flat seven note) prominently. These turnarounds are in the style of Yank Rachell. Rachell often tuned his mandolin below standard pitch - sometimes as low as E B F# C#. In this low tuning, a G shape chord sounds as an E chord. This allows easier string bending and the G shape (a friendly key on the mandolin) is used to play with a guitarist in the key of E (a popular blues guitar key.) The dotted rest lasts three quarter notes. Count *one, two, three* to start the measure.

The scale pattern on this and the previous introduction uses the open, third and fifth frets extensively. This recognizable pattern allows for quick memorization of the G blues scale.

This turnaround features a two note lick that is featured in *Yank's Blues* on page 14.

Here is a simple turnaround in the popular blues key of E. The sound of the lick is a sort of descending "yodel."

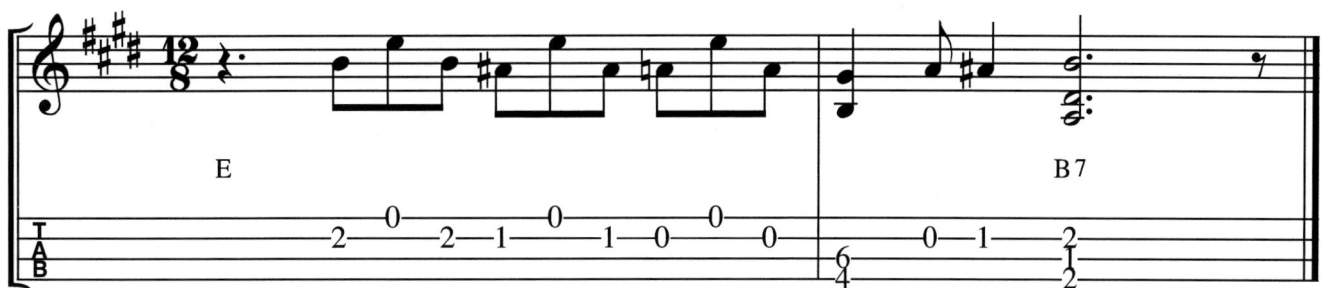

This turnaround is in A and uses three note chords.

This turnaround in D moves from the one chord (D) to the five chord (A) by ascending. This is sort of a reverse "yodel."

# Introductions

Blues songs are often introduced with four measure phrases like the ones below. Here is an introduction in the style of Johnny Young. The progression is 5 4 1 5. This introduction uses the D and G scales and is written in 12/8. Notice the D7 chord in the last measure.

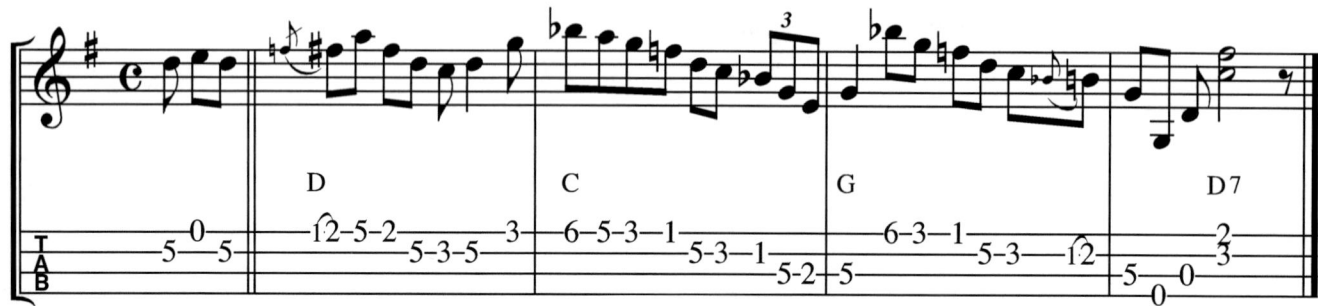

This introduction is in Charlie McCoy's style and is a 5511 progressions. Notice that while Young uses the second fret, first string F♯ note on the first measure in the example above, McCoy plays the first fret F natural in the same location. McCoy's use of the minor (flatted) third against the D major chord creates more tension while Young's slide to the F♯ releases the tension.

Here is similar introduction this time in the key of C. Notice this introduction is almost identical to the previous one except that it is "moved over" a set ot of strings from 3, 2 and 1 to 4, 3 and 2. The progression is 5 (4 5) (1 4) (1 5.) Chords in parenthesis receive two beats each.

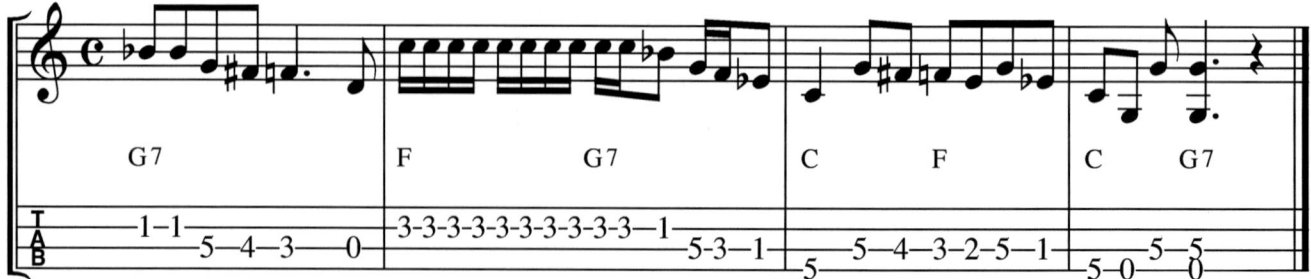

This Willie Hatcher style introduction is a 5 4 1 5 progression. In the key of D, it uses the D blues scale in measures 0-1 and G blues in measures 2-4. Measure four is the turnaround. This introduction is written in 4/4 time.

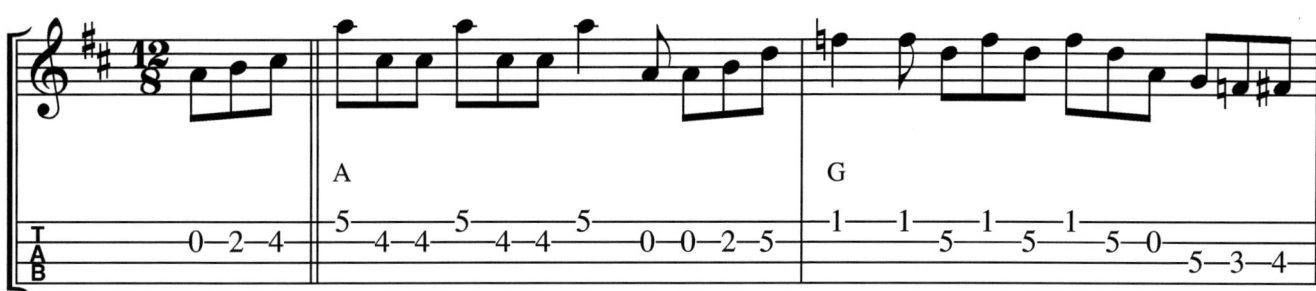

Here is a key of G introduction in the style of Carl Martin. The progression is 5 4 1 1.

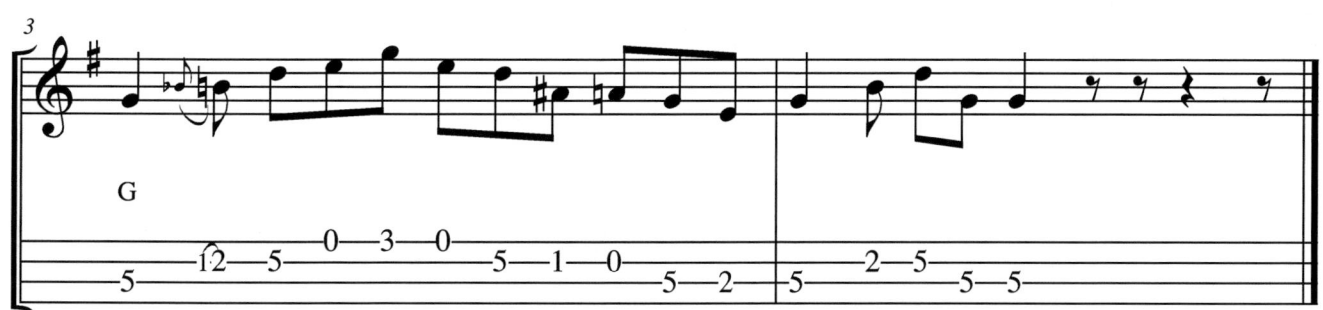

# Joe's Blues

This blues is based on a popular blues guitar riff. The turnaround in measure eleven requires a pick skip from the D string to the E string.

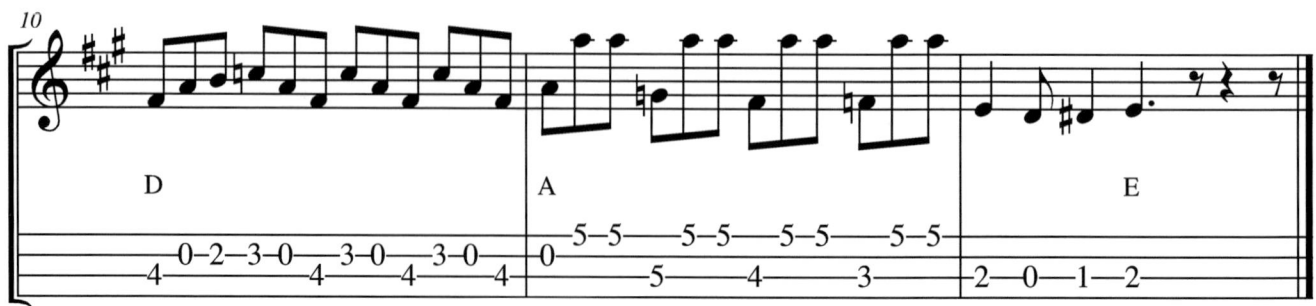

# Creating a Blues Solo

This blues is based on the popular 1934 *Milk Cow Blues* by Kokomo Arnold. This song was recorded by Bob Wills and other white bands in the 1930s and it has become a classic showpiece in many country music groups.

The basic 12 bar form follows this progression: 1 1 1 1 4 4 1 1 5 5 1 1. Below is the basic melody. The first two phases of staves one and two are the same except for the B flat note in measure nine. The top pair of staves contains the melody while staves three and four contains the mandolin introduction and fill licks.

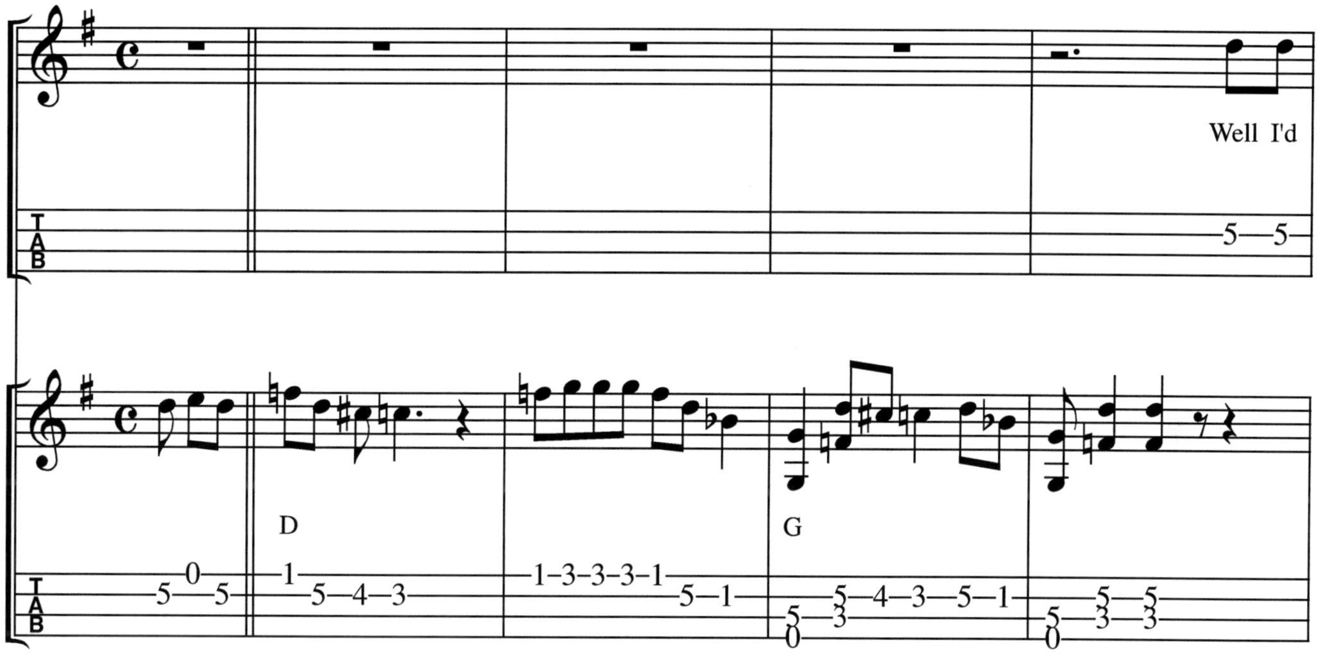

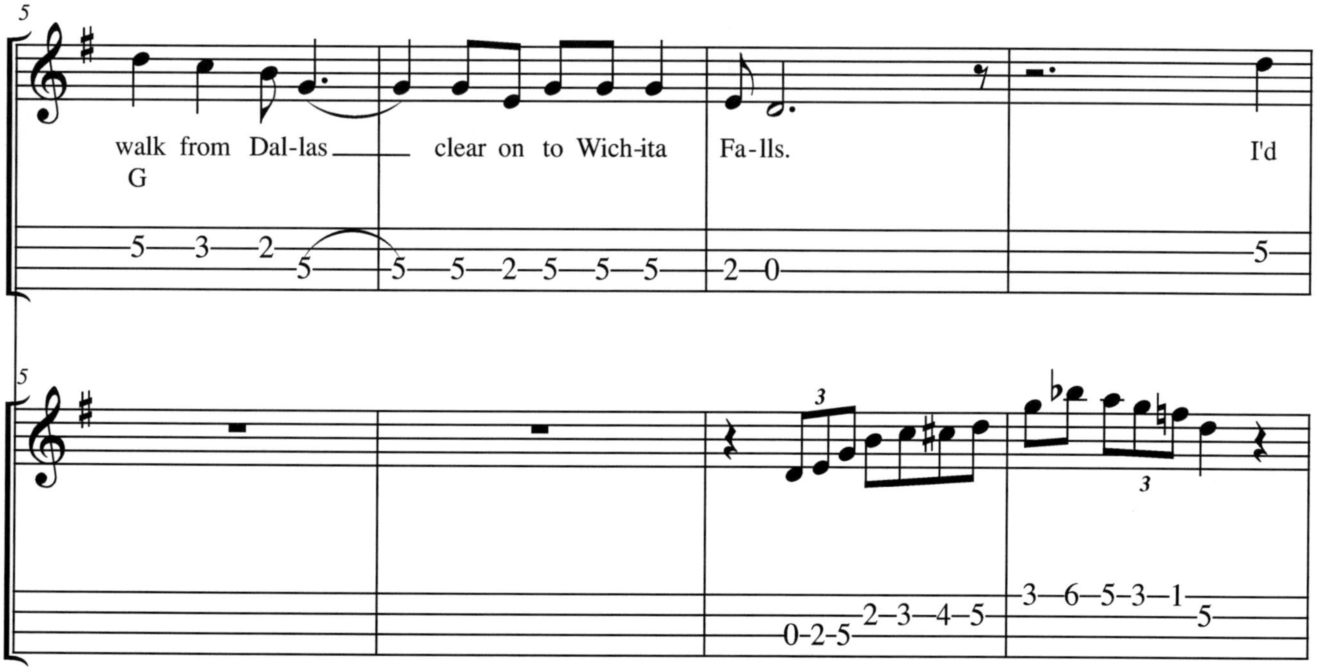

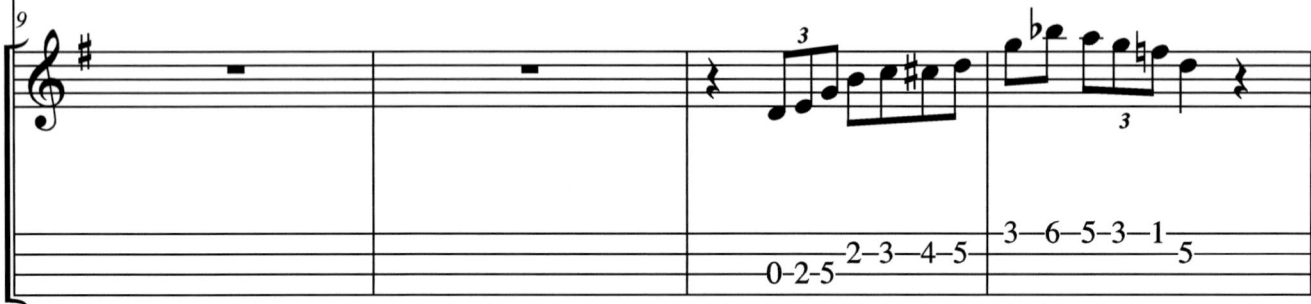
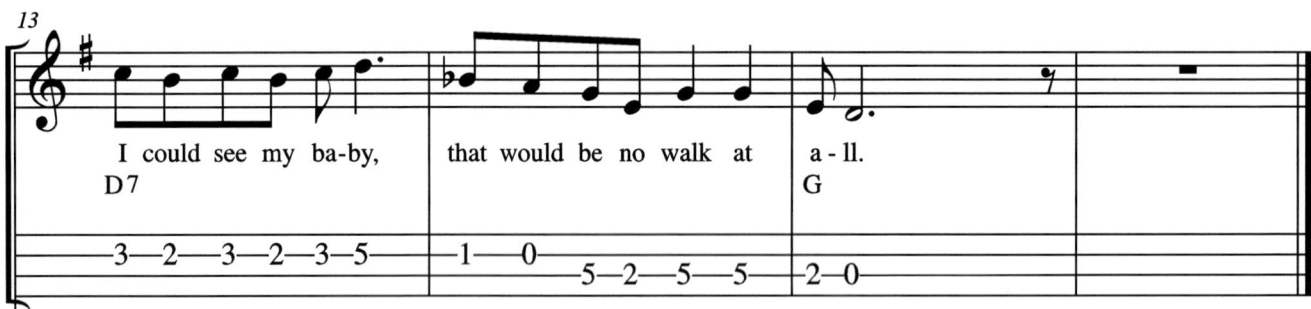
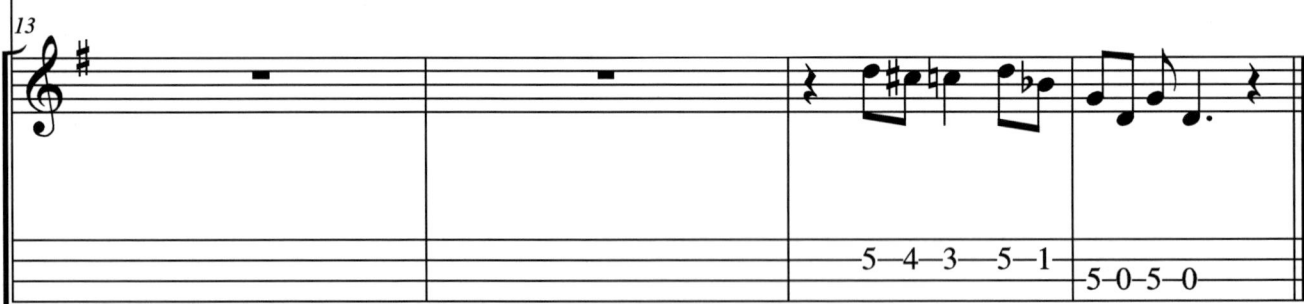

# Creating a Blues Solo - Part Two

The first thing to notice in the melody of this blues are the big "holes" in measures 3-4, 7-8 and 11-12. The first two "holes" are perfect places for fill licks. Since these measures are all during the G chord, the licks can be created from notes in the G blues scale. The lick in measure 4 ends on an F note, creating a G7 chord. In measure seven, we use the F (flat seven) note again. In measure eight, we use the flatted third B♭ and regular third (B.) The turnaround in measures 11-12 sends the progression back to the beginning.

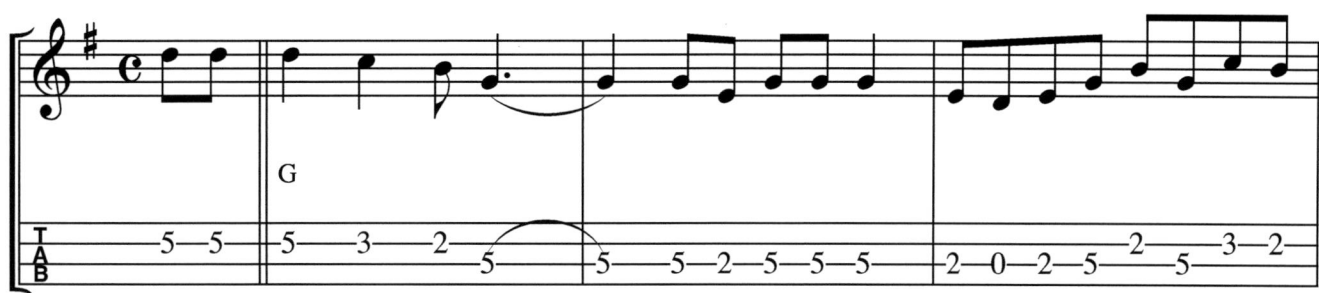

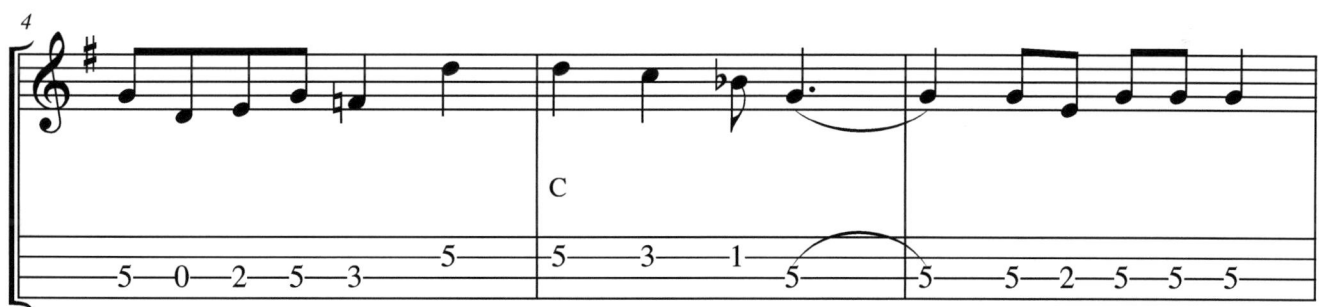

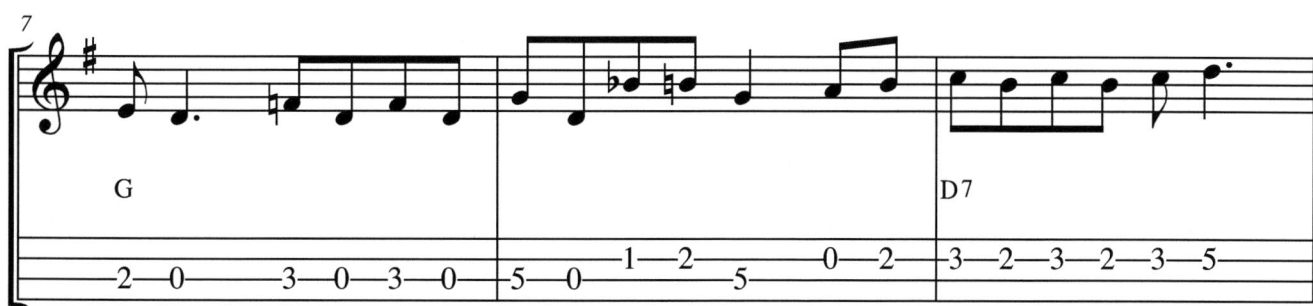

# Creating a Blues Solo - Part Three

The lick in measure one is a useful phase in many situations. The lick in measure ten uses several chromatic (consecutive half steps) notes in the G blues scale.

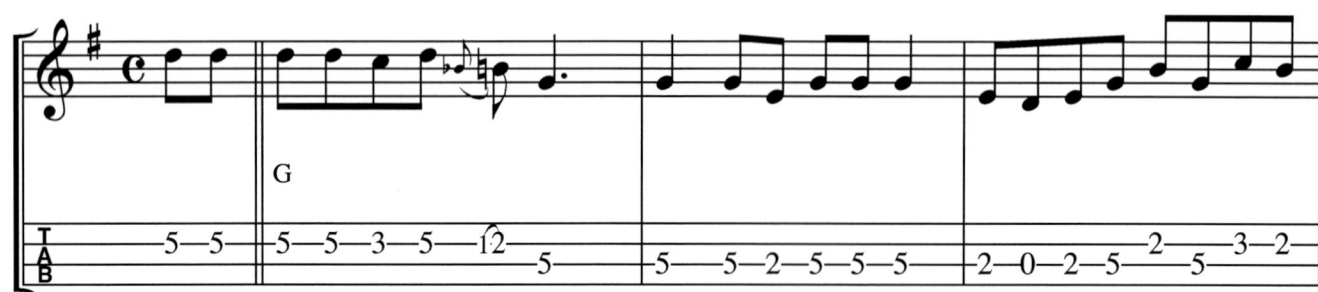
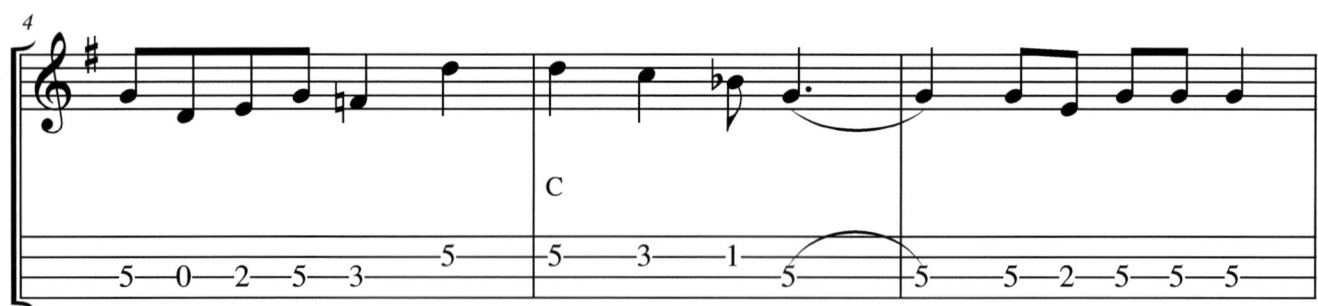

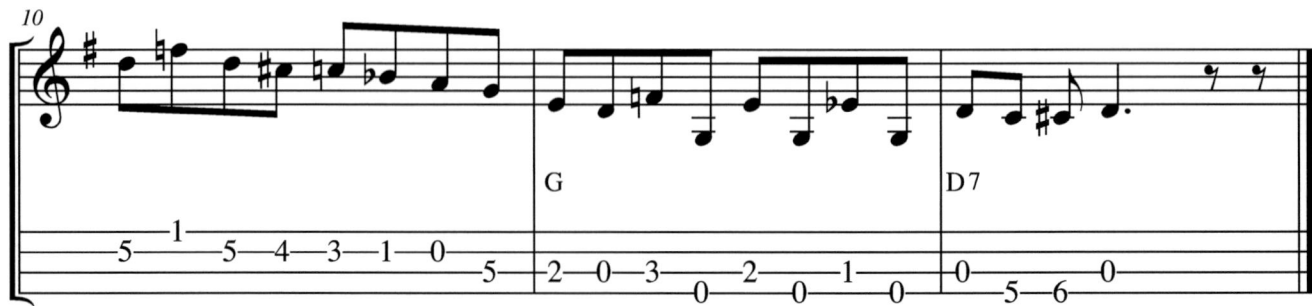

# Creating a Blues Solo - Part Four

This solo is a rough approximation of one played by Charlie McCoy. Notice he uses the B, C. C#, D note sequence throughout the solo. These four notes are played on the second string and are varied in time value and in placement. While the notes fit with the chords, there is no hint of the melody.

# Minor Blues - Saint James Infirmary

This traditional folk song is an example of a minor blues. It has been recorded by many including Cab Calloway and Louis Armstrong. Since the blues scale contains the minor third, it fits well over minor chords. While minor blues songs are not common, you should none-the-less be prepared to play one.

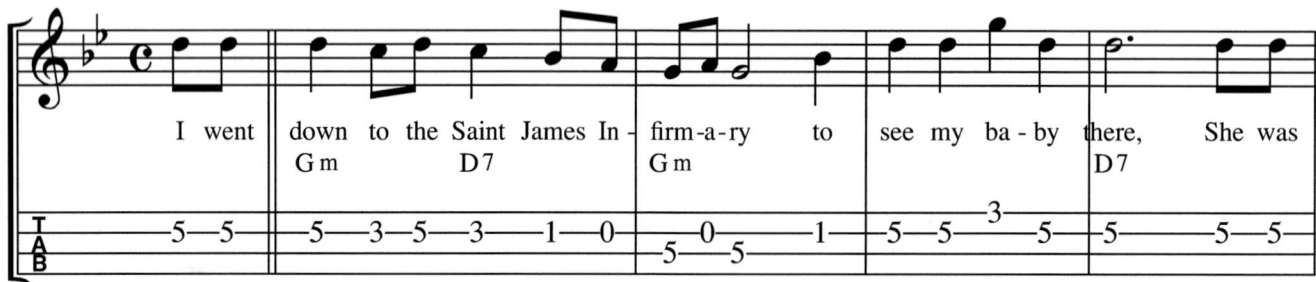

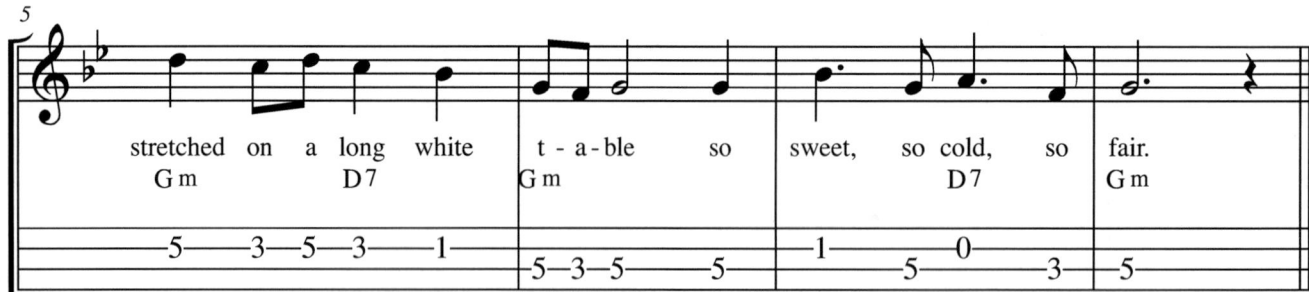

Here is the set of notes that appears in the melody of *Saint James Infirmary*.

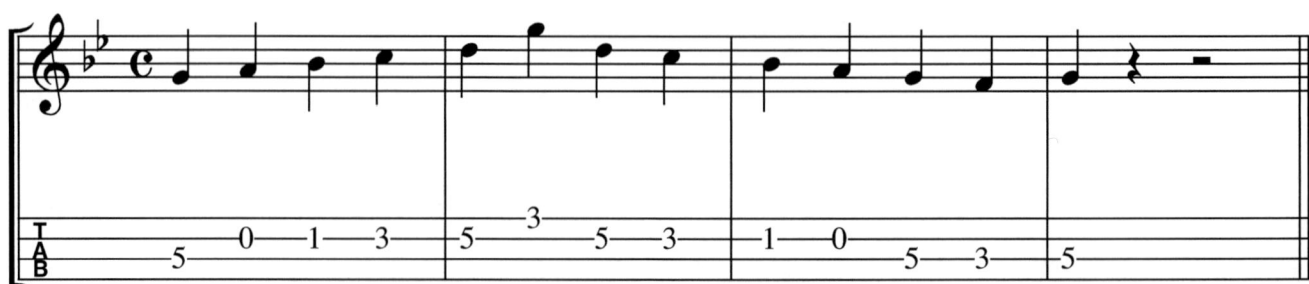

# Minor Blues - Saint James Infirmary Solo

The solo uses a few added notes from the blues scale. The notes in measure four come from the D scale with the added third fret (C) flatted seventh note.

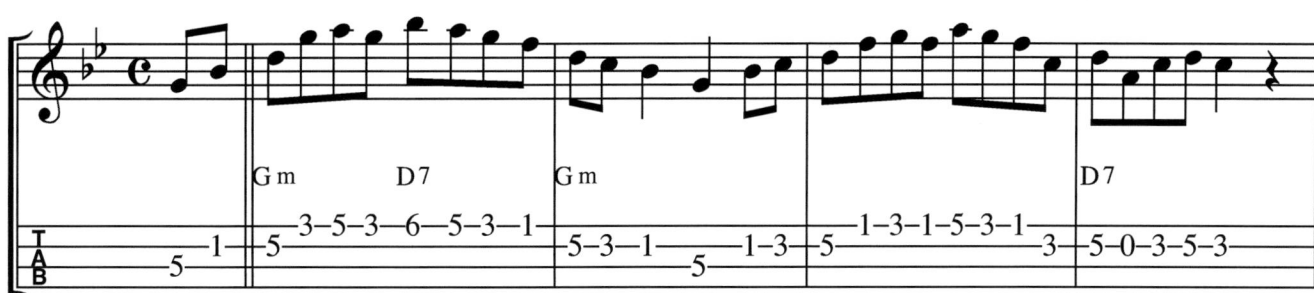

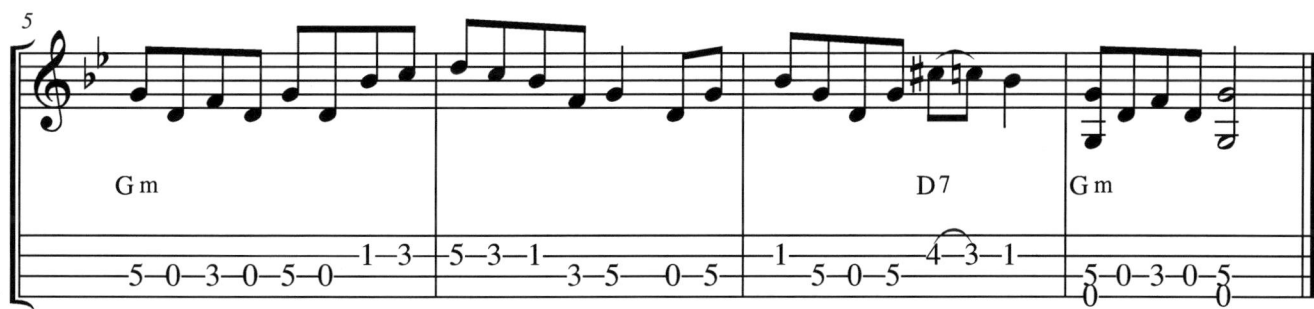

# Jazz-Blues Mandolin

Since the 1930s, numerous musicians have used the mandolin as a lead voice in western swing style and traditional jazz. Because jazz borrows many ideas from the blues, these players incorporated the blues sound into their solos.

Country comedian Jethro Burns was a talented jazz mandolin player who established himself as half of the comedy duo, Homer and Jethro. Jethro's brilliant mandolin playing was liberally sprinkled throughout the duo's many recordings from the 1940s to the 1960s.

This simple blues in C might be called a "riff blues" because of the repeating melodic riff in the melody. In jazz, many instrumental blues songs are written in this "riff" style. This unusual eight bar blues follows this form:

1 1 1 1
4 4 5 1

## Jethro's Blues

# Tiny's Blues

Western swing musician Tiny Moore played fiddle and mandolin with Bob Wills' Texas Playboys in the 1940s. He played a solid body electric mandolin with five single strings tuned C, G, D, A and E. Moore's initial move to single strings was prompted by the outbreak of WWII and rumors that mandolin strings might become unavailable. Moore grew to like the guitar-like sound and continued with this setup throughout his career.

Note the use of jazzy tones such as the ninth (F) in measure five and sharp five (C#) in measure nine. The jazz tones are identified by their relationship to the current chord, i.e. the F note in measure five is the ninth note of the E♭ scale.

# Jazz Blues Progressions

When jazz musicians play the blues as in *Tiny's Blues*, they often alter the basic chord progression to include more harmonic movement. One such alteration is to add a minor chord built on the fifth of a seventh chord. This progression:

G G G G7
C C G G
D7 D7 G G becomes:

G G G (Dm G7)
C C G G
Am D7 G G

The rhythm players can make these substitutions as well as the lead players. Another such substitution appears in measures seven through nine of *Johnny's Blues* on page 31. The original progression:

G G G G7
C VC G G
D7 D7 G D7 becomes:

G G G G7
C C (G Am) (Bm B♭m)
Am D7 G D7

Another common alteration involves the final two measures. In the standard progression they are:

G D7

Using a circle of fifths chord progression, the chords become:

(G E7) (A7 D7)

Finally, by adding a C major to C# diminished chord movement to this progression along with all the previously mentioned alterations, we get this highly altered blues:

G (C C# dim) G (Dm G7)

C C# dim (G Am) (Bm B♭m)

Am D7 (G E7) (A7 D7)

# Johnny's Blues

Johnny Gimble is a talented swing fiddler also known for his mandolin playing. His early career included a stint as a member of Bob Wills' Texas Playboys. He followed Tiny Moore in that group and therefore was very aware of Moore's approach. Gimble plays an electrified acoustic mandolin strung with four single strings tuned C G D A. When asked why he used this lower mandola tuning, Gimble quipped that the little E string sounded "too Tiny." This pun was an obvious reference to Moore's electric mandolin sound.

This jazz-blues is in the Gimble style. Notice the strategic jazzy use of rests and altered tones. The notes in measure two outline a G major nine chord and the notes in measures 5-6 spell a C11 and a C7♭9 chord. The G♯ note in measure 12 is a flat nine note. This solo is unusual in that it is totally within the mandolin range. Many of Gimble's solos have sections below the normal mandolin range. The chords in measures 7-9 are a jazz substitution.

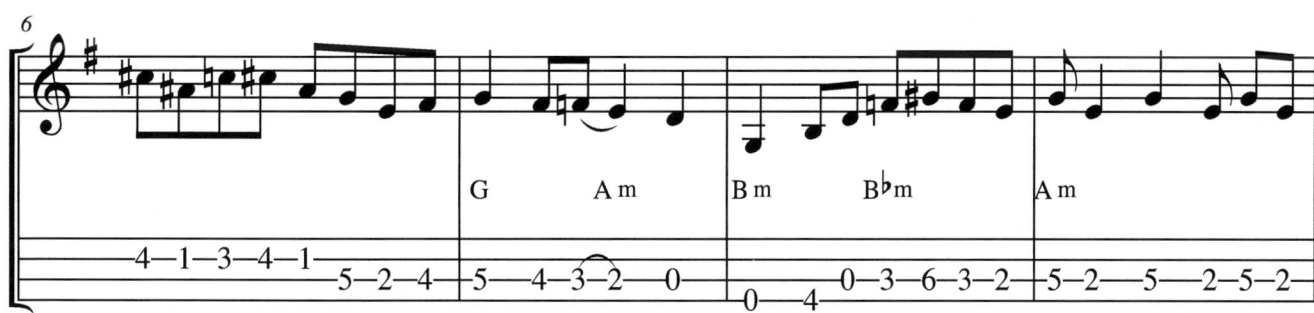

# Conclusion

Now that you have completed this volume, look for other books in the *School of Mandolin* series - bluegrass fiddle tunes, classics and Italian favorites.

# About the Author

Since 1985, Joe Carr has been a music instructor specializing in Bluegrass, Western Swing and Irish music in the Commercial Music program at South Plains College in Levelland, Texas. He is a director for Camp Bluegrass, a summer residential Music camp in its 23rd year (2009.)

In 1977, Joe joined the internationally known *Country Gazette* bluegrass band with banjo player Alan Munde and bluegrass legend Roland White. Joe appeared on three group albums, a solo album and numerous other recorded projects during his seven-year tenure with the band. In the 1990s, Carr and Munde formed a duo that toured extensively throughout the U.S., Canada and England and recorded two albums for Flying Fish/Rounder Records.

Joe has developed and appeared in over thirty instructional music videos for Mel Bay Publications and Texas Music & Video. He has written many instructional book/CD combinations for Mel Bay and has a growing number of DVDs available. Included are diverse titles such as *Western Swing Fiddle* MB20289BCD, *Mandolin Gospel Tunes* MB20554BCD and *School of Country Guitar* MB21645BCD.

Joe is a regular columnist for *Flatpicking Guitar Magazine* and *Mandolin Magazine* and is a periodic contributor to *Fiddler Magazine*. He is the editor for Mel Bay's webzine Mandolin Sessions. www.mandolinsessions.com

In 1996, the Texas Tech University Press published *Prairie Nights to Neon Lights: The Story of Country Music in West Texas* by Carr and Munde. Joe can be seen and heard at acousticmusician.com/JoeCarr.html